Lovely Nacuru.
with love
Toy key.
x x x

# Tony-Y-Not

# Tony-Y-Not

## The Last Drink

## Thomas Kelly &
## Co Creator Tracy McSeveney

BALBOA.
PRESS

A DIVISION OF HAY HOUSE

Balboa Press books may be ordered through booksellers or by contacting:

Balboa Press
A Division of Hay House
1663 Liberty Drive
Bloomington, IN 47403
www.balboapress.com
1-(877) 407-4847

ISBN: 978-1-4525-7532-2 (sc)
ISBN: 978-1-4525-7533-9 (e)

Printed in the United States of America.

Balboa Press rev. date: 07/02/2013

# Foreword

· · · · · · · · · · · · · · · · · · · · · · · · · · · · · · · · · · · · · · · · · · · · · · · · · · ·

**SIFA Fireside—30 years in Birmingham tackling homelessness, alcohol misuse and social exclusion.**

'I'm very pleased to recommend Tony's story to a wide readership as it describes his journey from being on the streets and in prison to becoming the socially aware and concerned citizen he is today, and does it in a thoroughly vivid and accessible way.

I think it's also important that it highlights the valuable work done by SIFA Fireside, a charity with over thirty years' experience of working with disadvantaged adults in Birmingham, in giving people self respect along with the practical support and skills to get their lives back on track. Each week SIFA Fireside has over 745 attendances at its daily 'drop in' sessions and serves 715 meals to people who are homeless or vulnerably housed. Last year we also worked in depth with more than 2400 people like Tony, helping them tackle health and addiction problems, stay away from the Criminal Justice system and find settled accommodation. For more information please visit www.sifafireside.co.uk and follow us on twitter @sifafireside.

**Most of all you'll find Tony's story a very good read!**

Cath Gilliver
Chief Executive
SIFA Fireside—48-52 Allcock Street, Birmingham B9 4DY
Tel: 0121 766 1700
www.sifafireside.co.uk

# Introduction
# Welcome to T& T Promotions

. . . . . . . . . . . . . . . . . . . . . . . . . . . . . . . . . . . . . . . . . . . . .

**Roll up, roll up!** We are here to tell you a little about this pair. A new dynamic pair; new to the scene and a pair to be watched for who knows what they will get up to. They are a mismatched pair of individuals if ever you saw, yet together, make a perfect match. 'T' stands for Tony & the other 'T' stands for Tracy. Some call them, double Trouble!

Tony is an Alcoholic in the truest sense of the word and when he gives you his word today he sticks by it. Now as for Tracy, well she has always been good to her word and is in fact an unknown creative writer who puts colour, emotion and brings words to life. She bring Tony's story of his last drink to life for all to read and appreciate and learn from his journey. He is an inspiration to all.

Tony has always had a good play on words and can rearrange them in the blink of an eye to create different words with different meanings. He puts love into all the words he makes and hopes that these words and his story carry wisdom and hope to others.

Tony's story has been told through Tracy for her to pass on to you. She puts her being into Tony's words and together they have created a book that hopefully will reach out to others. This book is about finding **peace, happiness, joy and most of all Hope!**

Together they have shared tears of joy and many moments of personal growth and happiness. It started with Tony's last drink and now the rest is for you to decide if you care to. Tracy & Tony have wrapped this book up with love and hope that you feel it, see and know it. Thank you for choosing to read this book. You will not only learning from this but you will also be helping others to, so . . . THANK YOU.

# Preface
# Words from Tracy

. . . . . . . . . . . . . . . . . . . . . . . . . . . . . . . . . . . . . . . . . . . . . . . . .

I met with Tony to talk about his book and to see if I were able to help him capture his story. The meeting was an experience to wonder at I can tell you! Sat in front of me in his flat cap and colourful waistcoat, he looked the true tinker. He even had that mischievous twinkle in his blue eyes that reflected his joy of life. His presence oozes energy and happiness. He walks with confidence and with his head held high and he does not miss a thing of what his happening around him or his environment. He behaves like a true gentleman and even compliments me on how radiant I looked.

He starts to tell me about what he wants to capture in his book, he talks so fast it is difficult at times to keep up with him. His thoughts and feelings of the past flow uninhibited from his mouth as he describes it in so much detail. A mental picture automatically is being created in my mind's eye as his story unfolds.

He is so appreciative of all that has been, all that will be and values every moment of the "now". He echoes my own words when he tells me **"All we have is now and we don't have anything else"**.

He says that his mind is empty and I know what he means. There is no self chatter going on in his head, no self talk to keep you trapped in your own world of thought. He is free to see, hear, feel and be a part of the world that continues on around us as we go about our business of living or should I say existing. There is no self doubt, no voice telling him what he should be doing. All there is stillness, an inner calm that enhances the feeling of being truly 'You'.

We are sitting here in a coffee shop in Birmingham surrounded by chatter and noise. People are eating and drinking whilst working on their laptops or on their mobile phones. We are surrounded by people caught up in the rat race and the world of technology. Most of them are not even aware what is going on around them and they are certainly not aware of this remarkable man sitting before me. Tony and I sit and talk captured by each other's words. We are aloof, or as Tony would say we are 'a-fool'. He has a knack of turning a word around so that it creates a new word and different meaning. Who are the fools in this scenario I wonder? We both sit relaxed and inner contentment is radiating from both of us. We are comfortable in our own skins and in each other's company and we both have stories to tell.

Tony is passionate about telling his story to the world and from the little snippets of information and detail of his experiences; I know his story will be a great one. A story that we all can learn from. I just hope that I can capture his essence and paint a true picture in words of is world, past and present. The words I will write will allow you to create your own picture of him and his story, I know that we all we create something different yet I have a feeling it will leave exactly the same impression on you as this man has left on me.

# Tony's Story . . . The Last Drink

"How the f**** did I get here!" this is what I said as looked down upon myself, looking at "me" through a different pair of eyes and from a different point in time. God I looked a sorry state in the pouring rain that early morning. I had been a married man with four children and a house and it was all gone! I looked up into the sky and cried **"God help me, I truly am an alcoholic!!"**

It's the 15th of August 2007, the rain is lashing down and a storm is brewing. Little did I know that my life was about to change. My mood was a true reflection of the weather as I sat there in the pub having just downed three pints of Scrumpy Jack. What a bloody sight I must have looked sitting there in dirty smelly clothes, a shaven head and only twenty pence in my pocket. I didn't care for I was with the love of my life. I sat there caressing the contours of the glass with rough hands that were dirty, grazed and bloodied and I became aware of a feeling of anger starting to bubble up inside me. I tried to ignore it so took another slug of my cider. I can feel the anger start creeping through my body and my thoughts. I can't stop it, it's coming, and I can feel it, an anger that I had never experienced before, oh no . . . It's here! It was like a force that I had no control over; it consumed me and was to take me on a journey of no return! All the anger throughout my life was bubbling up to the surface. The volcano was about to erupt. I start shouting and bawling at anyone who was listening or even not listening. I was screaming at the people who were my friends. They tried to calm me down, but that was never going to happen. I had never channelled my anger out on anyone; it had built up over time. Yes, I'd had flashes of anger in the past, but this was different; very different. **I WAS ANGRY**! I was spewing pure heated anger and hatred into that room. The anger was bubbling up and into the very path of my friends. I wanted them to call the police so that this pain and hatred would come to an end.

I staggered over to the snooker table and started throwing the balls in the air and head butting them as they came back to earth. I thought I was George Best. I felt no pain; it did not stop the hot lava from spewing from me. Blood was starting to trickle down my face as the force within grew bigger and stronger. I felt nothing but anger and wanted to be free of it! I reached out for anything that I could use to stem the flow; to stop the pain! I started even started head butting the stalls. I was shouting, fighting and no one was listening! No one was going to call the police . . . they had too much at risk themselves to do that. I was manhandled out of my watering hole by people who I have sat with for many years before and tossed out into the streets.

I stood there, cursing and swearing at the closed pub doors. Rain was penetrating my jumper and dirty clothes. Blood was pouring down my face like a lava flow from a volcano. I looked like a drowned rat that had been beaten with a stick. You can't get any lower than this.

I started to wobble up the street. I had nowhere to go; all I had were the clothes on my back which were now wet and blood stained with twenty pence in my pocket. Where **do** you go from here? I had to find somewhere, there had to be somewhere; there just had to be. I had no one to care for or care for me. My life was over. As I am staggering up the street, with my heart in my dirty black shoes that squelched as I walked, I saw a taxi draw up across the street and a lady put out by the taxi driver into the dark night alone. The very sight made me stop and my fuzzy brain starts to wonder. Something I might tell you has not happened for a long time. She starts crying and seems so distressed. The rain and the wind are only making the situation more unbearable for her. The wonder turns to realization and the alcoholic mist clears from my head, the anger subsides and I reach out to help the poor lass. She sees me approaching. She recoils at the sight and smell of me. Fear crosses her face. What have I become? I used to be a married man with a wife, four children and a roof over my head that I called home. I asked if she needed any help. She is still very wary of me and she sobs her tale of woe as we stand a foot apart in the darkness of the night. Eventually after speaking with her a little more and keeping my distance, she eventually lets me help her. She lets me call her boyfriend on her mobile and we start walking in the direction of where she lives. I walk 50 yards behind and kept calling out to her in the dark to check she was okay. She did not want to be seen with me. This is the level I have reached. No one wants to walk with me anymore. I am where I am today because I choose to be here. The love of my life has led me down a path I was happy to tread which led to nowhere, it was a dead-end. There was no life, joy or love along this path and the journey was becoming a very painful one. My mistress and I were coming to the end of the road. Just as I was hitting rock bottom, deep within me I hoped there was a way forward. There just had to be!

As we walked over Cuckoo Bridge, the boyfriend turns up and jumps out of the car. He takes her in his arms and all is well in her world once again. She is once again safe. I walk on and sit on the embankment. Tears start to fall down my face and I start to openly weep! Just as I start to slip down in to the darkness once again I hear someone call out to me. I look up. The young lady is walking back towards me! She thanks me and offers me a ten pound note. What would I, a drunken alcoholic, want with a £10 note when all he has is a twenty pence piece in his pocket? Whatever could I buy with that? I look at the money that she is holding out to me and then look back at her face and say thank you but no thank you! I didn't do it for the money; any human being would have done what I did. She asks me where I will go. I have nowhere to go!

She walks away and I slip back into my dark world and weep. The weather eventually brings me back to the here and now and I decide enough is enough so I walk up to and fall through the door of the police station and confess my crimes. Two big burly policemen grab me by either arm and they physically throw me out! I don't land on my arse but all fours! There is some hope after all.

Back out where I belong; in the cold wet dark night. The force within has again reared its ugly head as the night turns into day and in the early hours of the morning I walk into the middle of the main road to end the pain. Attention seeking some may say; a plea for help. I wanted someone to come and save me. This was the very moment that my life changed.

I drank myself onto the streets of Birmingham. I don't blame anybody for what happened in my life. I drank because I wanted to and I drank when I was drunk and then drank even more. I have not touched a drop of alcohol from that day to this. If I were to drink one drop of alcohol, it would take me straight back to where I was then and I like it where I am now. My life has not always been as wonderful as it is today, but I got here and I am here to tell my story and tell it I will.

I have looked back over my life and specifically focused on that particular point in time and thought about how I got there; why I got there and the reasons not to go back there. Before I go on, I want to take you back to the early hours of the 16th August and let you have an insight in to the steps that led me away from the drink!

Shouting and screaming at the world, venting my anger and frustrations at the rain and screaming, what became my most meaningful prayer **"God help me, I truly am an alcoholic!"** I was bundled into an ambulance and taken to hospital.

There were no life threatening injuries to speak of apart from the self inflicted ones; I was just a bloody nuisance to society. Left on a trolley I slept before being placed back out in the streets again! Yet life had already changed. I had for the last time sipped the bittersweet taste of my mistress and I had turned my back on her and walked away.

Back out on the streets again . . . . where do I go? Who will help me? I need somewhere to sleep, out of this bloody rain. I head to the hostel, a place of refuge. I couldn't get into the hostel. I had forgotten that I had been there before and I owed them £20. They would not let me in until I had seen the office staff, so I waited for them to arrive. I sat alone and dishevelled and just waited like a dog waiting for its master to let him inside to the warmth of the fire. I waited and I waited and eventually the reception area was opened up by the staff arriving on duty. They gave me the Housing Benefit From and I needed to give them twenty pounds. My heart sank; all I had to my name was twenty pence! Where was I going to get twenty pounds from? All I had were the clothes I stood up in, which was nothing to shout about I can tell you. I had been wearing these clothes for weeks and they stank! They stank more than stench itself. Who in their right mind would give me twenty pounds. I know I wouldn't especially looking and smelling like I did. My road ahead, my place to sleep, my next small step away from the drink and this life, if you could call it that, was blocked. It was a dead-end. I just wanted the world to end. Life was hard and the pain was too great. When I cried out to God to help me, I had thought just one thought, and that was "STOP!"

I had to stop, I needed to stop, and stop I did. I stopped drinking from that prayer onwards and here was my first test. A dead-end, my first challenge, my very first and I was stumped. Slowly a fuzzy thought came into my head. Who WOULD give me twenty pounds? Nobody was the first voice that answered me. I owed money to most people so WHO? My Wife? Yeah, she never had any money; she was always struggling to make ends meet. She seemed to be, by my logic, the perfect person to ask. So off I trudged with my head hanging low and my heart a heavy stone in my chest. It was a plan!

I walked in the direction of where I came. I was heading back to the other side of Birmingham and walking along Rocky Lane (how very appropriate) to the pub I had left the night before. A path leading me to my last drink! As I reached the same brow of the bridge where I had reached out to help another, a taxi pulled up alongside me and who should step out. A woman, she looked a little untidy and as she raised her eyes to me there was a look of surprise which quickly changed to contempt. It was my Wife. I was the last person she expected to pop up in her life at that very moment.

The relationship with my wife, when we were together, was very volatile and explosive. We were always arguing mainly due to the drink. There were times of love and times of hate; the times of love where very few and far between. The police were called many times to the house to remove me from the premises. The police seemed to always take the side of the female, although many times she was the aggressor. I hasten to add; for I do not blame her for it too was the alcohol that consumed her as well as me at that time.

The look she gave me was of one that said she wanted me out of her life! I was not wanted, not even the sight of me was welcomed. Anger spiked and I asked her for twenty pounds. She shoved the money in my face just to get rid of me. When I think back now to the relationships I had with my Wife and children I can l honestly say that we did not know how to love one another, yet deep down, I know we did. I am sure of that. I know now that I love them all so very much. Alcohol and drugs blocked my way but today God has removed the blocks and every day I will love them with all of my heart and soul.

I was amazed that she even had the money and was completely bowled over that she was stepping out of a taxi. Her life had moved on and so now had mine, for I now had the solution to the problem. Twenty pounds! I humbly took the money and headed back to the hostel. It was still raining and I was soaked to the skin. I felt nothing, absolutely nothing, how could l; I was lost and looking for a way out, a way forward away from this pain. After again trudging halfway back across Birmingham to get back to the hostel I presented the money. I had at least completed that test. Or so I thought!

I had spoken too soon. They took the twenty pound note from me but would they would not let me enter. I had not completed or had stamped the Housing Benefit Form. The test was not completed after all. They handed me the form and told me that I had to go to the Housing Benefit Offices the other side of town to get it stamped. This would prove to the hostel that their fee would be paid for putting a roof over my head. A place for me to lay my weary head. Many times before this, I had been evicted from hostels for the same reason as I was being evicted now. I had not had the form stamped! This was now becoming a shortcoming of mine and the pain was great.

The rain was still lashing down as I trudge the streets of Birmingham once again. I now have the form in my hand as I trudge on. A van pulls up alongside me and the very man I had been hiding from for week's steps out! Rumours were that he had been looking for me and that when he found me he was going to rip my head off. His face was red with anger. He had been a good friend of mine over the years, he had always been there to pick up the pieces and get me out of tight spots, of which I might add, were plentiful. He even paid my rent when times were hard. I looked at this red faced man and he looked like a man who was about to end my pain. So I turned and faced the inevitable. I had for weeks stolen from him under the cover of trust and in the name of friendship. I had worked for him, he had helped me and he had showed me nothing but friendship. All I did in return was to thieve from him. He had found out and now it was judgement day! Payback time.

He stood there in the rain shouting at me only an inch from my face and I just stood there! He screamed at me "Why? I am your friend? Why Tony? Why?" and all I could say with a shrug of my shoulders was "It's my head! I don't know; it's my head!" The drink stopped the pain, stopped the voices in my head. My sweet mistress just knew how to make me feel good, safe and how to forget. Her caresses were welcoming and warm and I know now, addictive!

His red mist started to clear as he started to see what sort of man he was talking to. A sorrowful, pitiful shell of a man. He saw what a broken man I really was, or so it seemed, a man at the end of the road. He asked where I was staying and when I told him that I was going to the hostel just down the road. He was horrified. The hostel did not have a good reputation even as a hostel for the homeless! It may have been as he put it 'a hole', but for the grace of God there was a bed. His anger turned to dismay as he calmed down and again he asked with a heavy heart "Why? I am your friend, why?" My feeble reply was "it's my head".

He told me to clean my act up and then go and see him. After all I had done, he was still there for me. It was in that moment that I started to learn the value of friendship for the very first time. True friendship and here it was standing right in front of me. I had stolen from this man, stolen right from him under his nose. I hadn't wanted to, I needed to, I just had to so I could be with my loved one! I could not break this pattern of behaviour; her spell over me was far too great. Little did I know, there was now a far greater force at play.

He started to step away from me and turn to go. I did not ask him for anything, I just wanted his forgiveness and being the great man he is . . . he forgave me! He is a true friend. Even today, he puts a roof over my head. He leaves me standing alone on the pavement as he drives off into the rain and I head off to the Housing Offices. I get my form stamped and head back to the hostel. This time I am given a place to lay my head and weary my bones.

For two days I shut myself away, sleeping and relieving myself in the sink for I just could not face the world. I was scared of the people who shared the hostel with me. They were people like me. These people were alcoholic, drug addicts and people with mental health issues. I was a chronic alcoholic and I was scared of me and people like me. This place just oozed with fear, doubts and worries. Yet I can now say that being a chronic alcoholic has been the best thing that has ever happened to me. I now live a life I am proud of and have a very privilege life style. I am at last appreciating what it is to be alive, mentally, physically and spiritually. Before now I had shut myself away from living and who I was.

On the very first day at the hostel I felt compelled to call my daughter. I had seen the public phone booth in the hostel reception and somehow, only God know how, I had memorized her telephone number. I decided I was going to call her. I was about to spend my last pennies in reaching out to someone, someone I had not seen for some considerable time. The very same daughter, who had given up on her pathetic father a long time ago. There had been some kind of closeness with my daughter unlike the relationship that I had with my sons. That relationship was always on the edge with my boys as I did not know how to truly relate with them; lots of arguing and shouting and not too much love. The only love I seemed to have then was the love for alcohol. Ironically, the public phone took twenty pence pieces where most these days only accept forty pence to make a call. I made the call, only God knows how. The phone was ringing and I hoped that someone would answer. It rang and rang and my heart fell even further as I realized no one was there! Then I heard her voice say "hello". My hopes and heart flicked into life as she spoke to me but within seconds she had passed the phone to her husband once she realized who was on the other end. He took my number and said he would call me back. It seemed he wanted to do the right thing and hey at least he was speaking to me. He was a man of his word and he called me straight back. He asked where I was and what I wanted and so I told him. I needed some money to get through the next week, even the next day as now I had spent all my money on making that call! So my twenty pence became twenty pounds.

My son-in-law came to the hostel to bring it to me. When he arrived he parked up the street far away from the hostel. He had my grandchildren in the car and he did not want, nor I, for them to see where I was staying. A place that only lost souls abide where you are given a bed, sheets, a blankets, and a bit of company. For now, that was all I could call home. I was frightened of the people there, people like me and what they would do to me or could do to me. I was too scared to even go to the toilet. For some, the torture of their own demons made them behave like caged wild animals. I have come to realize that people are not their behaviours and that was a hard lesson to learn.

After the third night of hiding away I ventured downstairs and sat in the day room with the others who where sweating, rolling, rocking and rattling. I was probably doing the same yet I was looking at them to take myself away from looking at myself. I now know that my God was with me at that moment for I was getting me through, albeit minute by minute. I was taking tiny steps to take me away from this world I had woke up and found myself in. I said to myself "Come on Tony, wake up, smell the coffee and get your life back together and when you do, come back make sure that you do something for those who can't". I didn't know it then, but I know it now . . . **hindsight is a gift of remembrance**! I can remember that day as if it were yesterday. Somehow I was slowly piecing my life back together. I seemed to be in the right place, saying the right things to the right people and the right things were happening. I had cried out to God the night of my last drink yet had never called on God after that . . . I don't think I was even consciously aware that I had even called out to him to help me.

I feared the hostel so much; I could not stay there any longer. The fear was becoming too great. I needed a place where I could feel safe. So I decided that I would go back to where I drank and squandered the little money had. Money that I should have spent on looking after and feeding my family. Money that was not even mine for I stole to drink and thought nothing of it. I don't steel today. As long as I could feel the glass in my hand and taste the sweet nectar which carried me away to a place of no feeling, a place that stopped my head from thinking, a place of peace and safety. I was happy. So I went back to the pub! I kept going back there day in day out, week after week sitting in the same spot drinking from the same glass feeling humble for now I was back in a place that I felt I belonged drinking pints and pints. Eight pints to be exact. Eight pints of lemonade! My last drink had lasted from the 12th the 15th August and had ended with those last three pints of Scrumpy Jack cider and here I sat in the same pub that I had been thrown out off feeling safe.

As time ticked on I started to gather some strength and decided that the time was right to face up to some people. I jumped a train to go and see my sister. I had treated her bad over my drinking years. I didn't care who I hurt in them days as long as I got a taste of and the comfort from my sweet mistress. The drink always came first, it was the only thing that was worth anything then or so I thought. To be honest not just with you but to myself, it came first, second and third; In fact it was the only thing in my life! I was oblivious to the destruction it was causing around me and how much it was really costing me . . . and I don't just me financially.

As I walked to my sister house my insides felt like jelly. Smelly, jelly belly Kelly that was me. I used to wobble up the street after I had a skin full and now I was wobbling for a completely different reason. I stood in front of her door and felt physically sick. I raised my hand with trepidation and knocked the door. I had upset a great many people and I was about to hopefully start making some amends. It all depended on the reaction I got when they saw me. If they closed the door in my face, I would not have blamed them. Many people would have for the things I did. It seemed a life time before anyone came to the door and my mouth was dry and my heart was racing. I was surprised that the banging of my heart was not heard by the whole neighbourhood. Eventually I heard someone coming to the door, I stood up straight and pretended to be a man. As the door opened the person was calling to someone behind them so they were not really concentrating on who was at the door. The laughter and smile slipped dramatically from their face as they turned to see who had actually come a visiting. The reaction was one of complete dismay. I was about to face the music and I was expecting what I got, what I deserved. She looked at me with sadness and a weariness that broke my heart. This was my sister and the look of mistrust hit hard, yet I know I had worked hard to deserve that look. I had earned it! She just stood there and the silence seemed to go on forever. We just looked at one another until eventually I raised my hand as if to stop any argument or ill feeling and asked if I could come in to have a wash, a change of clothes and possibly a sandwich. I asked her if she was able to do that for me. I told her that I was in a hostel and that I had not touch a drop of alcohol for a few days now. She stepped back and I thought she was going to close the door, instead she said for me to go in. She gave me what I had asked for and then we sat and chatted a little about what had been happening. My youngest sister was there too. She has since passed away, about 18 months ago, but it gladdens my heart to know at least she died seeing me a sober man and not an empty shell. I had a very special bond with my youngest sister and seeing her there made me feel very humble. We looked deep into each other's eyes, a look that spoke volumes. She reached out to me and we wept together in each other's arms. "How could I have ended up like this?" I asked myself, this was not a pretty sight and certainly one that I was not proud of. I only have to think back to that time now to remind myself the reason **why not** to go back there again especially in honour of her memory and for what she did for me. God gave me the strength to take one day at a time and still does today but there are some very special people who have been there for me too and I thank God they were and still are today. Before I left, my sister gave me ten pounds. I was now starting to get money and not one thought of drink had entered my mind. That was progress I can tell you!

On returning back to the hostel I quickly hid the money my sister had given me. I had to keep it safe for nothing was sacred when it came to the hostel. You had to be able to duck and dive in order to survive and by god I knew how to do that. I had ducked and dived all my life. Fear had been the driving force then and it was still so at the hostel but for different reasons. I had to face my fears, but I didn't know how to face them. I just knew I had to find a way.

For the next few days I sat quietly out of the way, watching the people around me, people who were the image of me. They too were running and trying to escape, they were no different from me. The drink took the pain away for a while, but it always came back!

My youngest sister had given me her number so I kept in contact when I felt the need and for most of my days I kept going back to the pub that I used to drink at. I seriously do not recommend other alcoholic to do this but for me it felt it was the only thing I could do. I had gone there so many times over a long period of time that it had become a part of me, a part of my identity. I was no longer drinking alcohol for lemonade was now my usual. I remember during this period of recovery asking someone who knew me back then "what was I like then?" and her comment was "you put yourself through torture darling!" I probably thought I deserved it, it was my pennants!

Every day I would sit drinking ten to eleven pints of lemonade. Madness I know, but it kept me sane. I would sit there and watch the world go by. I tormented myself by watching my wife with her new fella. I should have felt pain, and I probably did but I was not feeling it. I didn't feel anything. Absolutely nothing! I was just an empty shell of a man who felt nothing yet I was learning a very valuable lesson. I was learning humility and acceptance. I didn't know it then, but I can look back and see that was what I was learning. Life deals us many cards during our lifetimes and it's what we learn from these events that is important. I was just starting to wake up and take notice and my education was about to begin.

Six weeks had passed and still not a drop of alcohol had touched my lips. I had by now saved a little bit of money and decided that I was going to treat myself to a new jacket which I had seen in the British Heart Foundation Charity shop. I was starting to pay attention to my appearance which was a sure sign I was going in the right direction. I remember buying the coat for five pounds and someone at the hostel offered me thirty pounds for it and a lump of dope in exchange for it. I believe that if I had accepted their offer, which only a few weeks before I would have snapped their hand off, it would have taken me straight back to the drink. I was not willing to take that chance. No way was I going to sell the coat off my back! Not now. Not ever!

For weeks I kept myself aloof, sitting contemplating life and inwardly searching my soul and looking for answers. People would come up and chat to me asking how I was and how I was keeping. There was one chap that was keeping count of the days I managed to keep away from the drink! I would often smile and mutter some words in response. If I had been honest with them as to how I was feeling they would have run a mile. Standing outside the pub one night whilst looking to the skies for inspiration, I asked a chap "Is this as good as it gets?" his response was that it gets better! He was right! Life does get better, life gets good and you start to experience joy for living.

For some, we have to stand before the abyss of hopelessness and darkness before we can appreciate the light and joy of living in the moment. It is amazing what pain people will tolerate and endure before they decide to change. Some people never make that decision even when the pain is great. For what purpose do we deny ourselves happiness and joy? For what reason do we feel that we are not worthy of a life of wonder?

You don't have to be an alcoholic to lock yourself away from finding happiness, you only have to look at society today and see that so many people are just existing and not living. I thank God that my life has been like it has because the path I have trodden has taken me to hell and back and now I can see with my eyes, hear with my ears and feel with my heart. It's been worth the journey and tomorrow is another day. Another new day, one of learning, exploring and laughter. I can honestly say that I am a graduate of the University of Life and I am working towards my Honours.

My life was starting to develop some stability when I recalled the conversation that I had with a dear friend. He had told me to clean my act up and then go and see him. So I did! He had said that he would wipe the slate clean so I gave him a ring and he invited me in to his home. For the very first time in a long time, I was being invited and welcomed into a home. He introduced me to his family, cooked me a meal and offered me some work. By this time I was looking and smelling a lot fresher!

The work was repetitive factory work, boxing stuff up. It was work and it was keeping my hands and mind busy and taking me further away from the drink. I earned £34 a day. It wasn't about the money; it was payback time and I was doing it willingly. I was paying him back for what I had done to him in the past. I was doing the work to show him the gratitude I felt towards him for being a true friend.

Time went on and I started to accumulate a little money. I was stashing it away and not a thought of spending it on alcohol crossed my mind. I was still going to the pub every day, which again I must stress is not a great thing to do if you are an alcoholic. Things were getting better each day and then out of the blue, I was offered another job. Opportunities where starting to present themselves. I was asked if I wanted to be a night caretaker of a hotel in Lichfield. Me a caretaker! What, being left alone in a hotel at night with no one around to see what I was doing with an empty bar to patrol in the quiet hours of the night with all that alcohol in easy reach. Left in charge in a position of responsibility and trust. I was given the keys and a chance to prove myself worthy. I didn't drink and only God knows how I did that, for I wasn't even praying at the time, but someone was looking out for me, providing the strength and willpower to keep me away from temptation. Or was I in prayer?

I bought myself some new clothes to start the new job. This job was taking me further away from the hostel and it was a godsend. Sometimes after work I would go and spend some time with my youngest sister. Our relationship was blooming. She would often call me just to tease and torment me. I remember one Friday she called me and asked if I would go over and cook her a curry. I was quite a good cook even though I say so myself! Of course I went and cooked for her and I stopped the whole weekend. We had talked so much that on the Monday morning the curry was still sitting there untouched. She later told me that she was not that keen on curry after all and that she had just wanted an excuse for me to go and see her. Little did she realize, she did not need an excuse she only, had to ask and I would have been there. We had a very special bond and it was strengthening with each day that passed. I started to live with her and she used to leave me three pounds on the side. It was her way of supporting me along my journey. I was thankful for her gesture, not for the money but the thought behind the gesture. The act of giving is so much more than the gift itself.

Living at my sister did bring problems of their own. He boyfriend was someone I had taken a gun to in the past. I had hated him for the way he had been treating my sister during his dark times. I had wanted to kill him. I really mean kill him! I wanted to put bullets in him. That was then and this is now. He too was an alcoholic and if he were to need my help now I would be there for him.

I have travelled a long way and learnt many a lesson along the way, and am willing to share my wisdom and help others along the way. During my days of drink, it was probably the same for him, I can't speak for him, I can only tell you how I felt and behaved. But as an alcoholic you do not have rational thoughts and feelings and your behaviour is only a mirror of the torment within. Sometimes you will do anything for the pain to go away . . . even if it's only for a moment, but you will do anything! Yes even kill. God must have been in the side wings that day for something stopped from taking that fatal step.

So you will quite understand that this offer of a roof over my head was not an easy act for my sister to perform. Slowly fences were mended and bridges built and again I was learning humility once again. I was facing up to my actions of the past so that I was no longer kept a prisoner by them. Life moves on and so had I. I refused to be held captive by my old life. That Chapter of my life had been closed. A new chapter had begun and I was eager to keep turning the pages.

My little sister was such a giver. One day she brought me a bus pass! She was such a kind women. I can never repay the love and support she showed me. I have vowed to myself and to her memory never to touch another drop of alcohol ever again. It wasn't until I stopped drinking that we told each other that we loved one another. My love for her is now deeper than love itself. She may be asleep in the safe protection of Heaven waiting for me, yet I can feel her love for me around me like a soft warm blanket nearly every day. I feel her presence some days and it gladdens my heart that we did get an opportunity to share the love we had for each other and say those words with true meaning behind them. God bless you little sister, sleep safe and one day we will be together again.

Unbelievably, I was offered yet another job. Bar work which meant that I would not have to work nights all the time. An alcoholic working behind a bar!! Don't try it as it may not work for you, but it did for. I was serving other people the sweet taste of my long lost mistress, and not once was I tempted by her. My obsession for the drink had taken on a new guise . . . a beautiful woman. I was hypnotised by her and my obsession for her took me further away from the old style Tony. This woman was taking interest in me. Not that long ago people would not walk along side me never give me the time of day.

Whilst I was working at the bar they held a charity night for S.I.F.A (Supporting Independence from Alcohol). Little did I know, but in years to come I would actually be on that Charities pay role! Funny really how things enter your life and at the time seem to have no meaning or purpose and then just like a germinating seed, it breaks through the surface and is given the nutrients that are required for growth. The charity came into my awareness and my higher power was guiding me towards my destination and my future. When the timing is right, the seedling breaks through the surface and reaches for the sky.

Since having my last drink my senses were coming back into action. I was no longer numb or immune to the energies around me. I started to feel "resentment" around me which made me feel uncomfortable. I did not like the emotions that were bubbling up from this feeling and had just started to realise that we all have choices. So I decided to leave. Yes this would seam like I was taking backward steps when in fact I was taking major strides forward. I was taking action not just sitting back and taking what was being dished out.

Change requires action and I was well on my journey of change and no-one or thing was going to stop my progress. Three days prior to me telling them where to stick their job I had been speaking with a man who was in the process of interviewing for a bar manager in a new pub that was about to open. He had given me his telephone number as he had wanted me to sell some watches for him. Not legit I might add. Hey ho I still had a way to go yet. At least I was going in the right direction a little detour now and then was ok as long I was heading in the right direction. The watches were stolen. I called him about the sale of the watches the day I was about to jack it all in. He offered me a job! The manager who they had taken on had let him down and if I wanted it the job was there for the taking. As one door closes another opens. I was now a manager of a bar. Me of all people, I had never managed anything in my life well apart from managing to lose everything to drink. I now had a new job and a place to live above the bar. I became the life and soul of the party. Laughing and joking with the clientele. The greatest known host to mankind. I would chat up the ladies, boogie on the dance floor strutting my stuff for all to see. Laughter followed me around the room touching all in its path. Yet when I climbed those stairs to my room I left all the joy, laughter and bravados behind me. I had become the great pretender. With every step I climbed my heart got heavier and my inner light diminished. I was not climbing the stairway to heaven; I was climbing the stairway to hell. The loneliness was crippling me and destroying my soul. Lost in my world of sadness, I cried, weeping sorrowfully with my heart heavy with remorse.

In those hours of darkness I could hear the call of my old love and her sweet menacing lullaby ringing in my ears, tormenting me with promises of peace and warm loving arms and her velvet soft touch to make it all better. Her soft call was tempting yet the sound of silence was deafening and I turned back to the darkness and wept. I should have won an Oscar for my performance during that time, for I could be in the pit of despair wailing like an Apache in full war cry and stop just like that when called by someone from the bar requiring my assistance. Within seconds I could change my war face paint to that of a clown and with each step back down those stairs the more in character I became. The transformation was unbelievable. No-one knew or was it that no-one cared to notice. Many people in the pub used to make fun of the funny man and that was ok by me for at least I had somewhere to live and a job!

The owner of the pub used to like to play the "big I am". He was a regular user of coke and this had a major affect on his behaviour towards people and me. This was the sort of environment I was living in where drugs and alcohol ruled. Emotions were starting to swirl around deep within and I was aware of resentment bubbling up to surface. Sometimes he would push me so hard I would be peering over the edge . . . the edge where I really wanted to kill him. This was an emotion of the past and of the old Tony. I was not prepared to revisit those old haunts especially for him.

I had tried the coke scene really to be part of something, to see what it was like. I wanted to know what people got from it, I needed to know and once I knew I stopped. It was during this challenging time I started taking myself and others to the Fellowship. I should have been serving drinks to many of the people I had illuminated the path of redemption to!

Friendships started to develop and I became friends with a lot of ladies whilst living over the pub. I was seeing eight to nine different ladies at any one particular time. Some may call it charm; I would call it a gift, a special way with the ladies. Before you jump to the wrong conclusion, I was not a stud I was a friend, someone to talk to and someone who would listen. Little did I know that I was not the only lonely person around! When you are in that lost world friendlessness everywhere you look, people seem to doing okay and it seems to you that they would never understand the meaning of abandonment.

One lady thought her house was haunted and I was helping to convince her that it wasn't. Another lady I was emptying her bins. I was just doing good, good and more good making up for the times I had done dastardly things. Again I assisted the Charity that plays a massive role in my life today and held a couple of charity nights. One of which was on 31st October 2009, Halloween. Four years on I am now employed as a Support Worker with that same charity exactly to that date!! Spooky . . . very befitting for the time of year.

Other things were happening during this time although things were not improving with the owner of the pub and then just after Xmas he called me to tell me that there was no longer a job for me. I had to move out. I could hear the glee in his voice. I had been as much a thorn in his side as he had been in mine. I was one of the few people that really ever stood up to him. Power of self is a great thing. Seeing that he was in theory putting me out on the streets he had the decency to offer me a place to rent. I told him that I was okay and no thanks. If I had been honest I wasn't okay but no way was I going have him as my landlord!! No way, I would rather be back at the hostel than that. They say that pride comes before a fall and you know what, I was prepared for whatever.

After putting the phone down I quickly picked it up again and called my trusted friend. After explaining my predicament he informed me that he had no work for me but that he may be able to help with a roof over my head. In the garden of an old Victorian house was what you would call a type of annex that was built at the back of the property. He was putting on the market that day, but said if I fancied taking a look he would delay doing that until I had seen it. He said that it was mine for the taking if I wanted it, I didn't need to put any deposit down or anything like that, I just needed to take a look. No one had ever lived in it and when I saw it I knew I had come home. It was like it had been sitting there waiting for me.

Four years on it's still very much home and I love it! My safe haven sits on Orchard Road in an orchard surrounded by apple trees. To think five years ago I was living on the streets smelling of the stench of apples and now I am sitting pretty smelling the sweet scent of apples. I had gone from walking the streets of Birmingham to get my Housing Benefit form signed, meeting my friend on route, to now where the housing benefit pays my dear friend. I now have a job so I will be paying towards my own rent and that feels so good.

So I was now leaving the pub with HOPE. Many of the people I had met since my last drink have offered me a roof over my head. I would never have to sleep in a hostel again. I live with the knowledge that if I knocked on the door looking for a place to lay my head there are people out there that care and would reach out to me in my time of need. Mind you, if they heard me snore they would probably never offer me a bed ever again.

When I went to the Housing Office with my form there was a little voice in my head that wanted me to ask whether they owed me anything with regards to back payment for rent. I had used my friends sisters address in the past a place of residence even though I had not been stopping there and had agreed with her that we would split the rent between us. Here I was asking them if they owed me money when last time I had owed them. Things have changed since then and it makes me realize just how far I had come especially when they told me that they had just sent a cheque out to me in the post for the back rent. The cheque was for £3911.00! Two days prior to this I had lost my job and the roof over my head and now I was heading home with a substantial amount of money in my pocket. Change occurs even if we are not aware of it. It is like a big wheel. It just keeps on turning.

Being a man of my word, I went round to my friend's sisters to pick up the cheque. Her address had been the last address I had been registered too. I am not sure she would have contacted me about the cheque arriving, but I knew it was there. Whilst sitting in the car after cashing the cheque she was really mad and moody with me. To her money was everything. She told me that money was the only thing that drove her. I took eleven pounds from the bundle of notes and passed her the rest. Money drives her for whatever reason. She probably has a story of her own to tell, but this story is about my journey and not hers.

We all have choices and I chose to let her have the money. You can choose to avoid situations or go with them, the choice is ours to make. The most blessed thing in my life right now is the feeling of love. I have the feeling of nothingness in my head, and an overflowing feeling of love in my heart. I have my God's love.

**I have learnt to live life in sobriety and beyond.**

Beyond the beyond and beyond.


## From Wikipedia, the free encyclopaedia

**Sobriety** is the condition of not having any measurable levels, or effects from mood-altering drugs. According to WHO "Lexicon of alcohol and drug terms . . ." **sobriety** is continued abstinence from psychoactive drug use. Sobriety is also considered to be the natural state of a human being given at a birth. In a treatment setting, sobriety is the achieved goal of independence from consuming or craving mind-altering substances. As such, sustained abstinence is a prerequisite for sobriety. Early in abstinence, residual effects of mind-altering substances can preclude sobriety. These effects are labelled "PAWS", or "post alcohol withdrawal syndrome". Someone who abstains, but has a latent desire to resume use, is not considered truly sober. An abstainer may be subconsciously motivated to resume drug use, but for a variety of reasons, abstains (e.g. such as a medical or legal concern precluding use). Sobriety has more specific meanings within specific contexts, such 12 step programs, law enforcement, and some schools of psychology. In some cases, **sobriety** implies achieving "life balance.


## My Steps to Recovery

I cried out on the streets of Birmingham outside a hostel, "God help me I am truly an Alcoholic". I did not know it then, but that was my **first**

**step on the rocky road to recovery. Accepting what I was and what I had become, was probably the hardest of them all**. There was no longer anyone around for me to impress, not even a group of drunks. There was just myself, stripped to the bone, a mere shell of a man. That's how my life was back then. Put me in charge and that's where my thinking took me.

The **next stage of my journey was my First Step in the 12 Step Program in the Fellowship. I live by this program and do so still today as it enables you to live your life one day at a time, away from the first drink.**

I have through the guidance of this Program, come to believe a power greater than myself has restored me to sanity. Looking back to the time when I cried out to God, he has restored me to sanity. I would not be here today but for the grace of God and the Fellowship. On a daily basis I hand my life over to a god of my understanding to take care and guide me through the day. I had over a lifetime, been in Care of the Local Authorities, the prison system and under the thumb of my wife. They had done me no good. Five years on I am being looked after by an invisible force whom I choose to call God. I feel free as a bird and am starting to feel my way through life. That was my Third Step and any grateful alcoholic such as I, should not drink any God given day and I am truly grateful for all I have today.

The next step for me was making an inventory of all the wrongs that I have done and to share those with another human being and God. I have not done this fully as yet, well not the Fellowship's 'Big Book' way, but I am entirely ready to do so. I have shared my most intimate secrets with another human being and I have shared the wrongs that I have caused with other people, my Sponsor and a Priest within the Fellowship. I am continually doing sharing these wrongs on a daily basis. I always humbly ask God to take away my short comings. These, I believe, are things that I don't do which I should do. i.e: open up a bill and pay it rather than pay the money while worrying and thinking about being evicted.

To me, righting the the wrongs that I did to other people should be next. Such as stealing, lying and cheating. Making a list of all the people whom I have harmed over the years and to make amends to them <u>all</u>. Make direct amends wherever possible. An example of such action already taken was when I went out to see my sister's boyfriend and took him her ashes.

She had previously passed away two years ago. I put her ashes into a container, and then carried them in a bag. I then knocked on his door. This man was someone I had previously resented. I had taken a gun to him and was prepared to kill him! This was during the time when I was lost in my own world of madness. It was the for the grace of God and my wife at the time, that somehow broke through that fog of madness which prevented me from carrying out this act of destruction and self-destruction. Two years on and here I was to make amends. We sat, we talked, and we cried together. I asked him if he would like my sister's ashes and handed him the bag. He cradled them and wept. It was as though he had taken her hand and she was there with us. We wept together. When it came time to leave, I told him that if he ever needed me, for I believe he is what at a place that I once had visited, that I was there for him. Forgiveness and self-forgiveness is the way forward. I always try to be conscious of my behaviour and willing to say sorry if ever I offend, hurt or upset anybody. By doing this, it clears my conscience.

I pray daily and throughout the day. I take time to reflect through prayer, meditation and stillness so to come closer to God. This way I am able to ask for his guidance. To be shown the right next thing to do for the next person that I come into contact with. I have had a spiritual awakening as a result of these Steps and the words before you and I hope that awakens within you and takes you to a place of peace.

I bring this message to other alcoholics and that is to keep these Principles in all of your affairs in life. I believe that my awareness today is aware of 'me'. All I have to do is to hand my life and my will, with complete abandonment, to God and to do for others what they cannot do for themselves. God will do for me what I cannot do for myself so on a daily basis I live within the light of the Twelve Steps.

**One day at a time.**

**In the name of our Lord and Saviour, sweet Jesus.**

**Amen.**

## **The Original Twelve Steps**

- We admitted we were powerless over alcohol—that our lives had become unmanageable.
- Came to believe that a power greater than ourselves could restore us to sanity.
- Made a decision to turn our will and our lives over to the care of God *as we understood Him.*
- Made a searching and fearless moral inventory of ourselves.
- Admitted to God, to ourselves, and to another human being the exact nature of our wrongs.
- Were entirely ready to have God remove all these defects of character.
- Humbly asked Him to remove our shortcomings.
- Made a list of all persons we had harmed, and became willing to make amends to them all.
- Made direct amends to such people wherever possible, except when to do so would injure them or others.
- Continued to take personal inventory, and when we were wrong, promptly admitted it.
- Sought through prayer and meditation to improve our conscious contact with God *as we understood Him,* praying only for knowledge of His will for us and the power to carry that out.

- Having had a spiritual awakening as the result of these steps, we tried to carry this message to alcoholics, and to practice these principles in all our affairs.

## **<u>My daily prayer</u>**

"Lord I open my mind to the knowledge of your will for me and for the power to carry it out. I'm Tony and I'm an alcoholic and my life was unmanageable. I have come to believe a power greater than me has restored me to sanity. By handing my life over to the God of my own understanding, the father the son and the Holy Spirit I can have a daily reprieve from Alcohol. By remembering my last drink that I drank at the Sportsman in Saltley, a place where my dad used to frequent as I did before and afterwards on many occasions. It was for the total effect, I did not know it then but I do now.

Looking back in hindsight which to me is a gift of remembrance and by remembering my last drink and by asking thee God to keep me away from my first drink because I do not want to go back to that way of living; lying, cheating, stealing and all the things that come from drinking.

God I offer myself to thee to do with me hast thou will relieve me of the bondage of self that I may do your will and take away my difficulties and they may bear witness to those I would help with thy power thy love and thy way of life may I do thy will a always Amen.

My creator, I am willing that you should have me good and bad and I pray that you may remove every single defect of character which stands in my way of usefulness to you and my fellows so that I may better do thy will.

If I have hurt anybody in my thoughts ways or actions I am deeply sorry but I am human and apt for mistake.

I pray for everyone inside and outside the Rooms of the Fellowship. The poor, the needy, and mental health with no exclusion. I am honest, open minded and willing and I pray for the physical, mental and inner strength to do thine will at not mine be done.

I need not fear today as fear is false evidence appearing real or face everything and recover and I choose to install them within me as I have a very healthy respect for alcohol. It has it has rendered me to my knees Lord. I have embraced people, places and things today and to the best of my knowledge I have lived the way the good Lord would have wanted me to do with love in my heart for my neighbours, and I ask this in the name of Jesus Christ, Amen.

Our father who art in heaven hallowed be thy name thine kingdom, thy will be done on earth has it is in heaven give us this day our daily bread and forgive us our trespasses as we forgive those who trespass against us and lead us not into temptation and deliver us from evil for thine is the kingdom the power and the glory forever and ever Amen.

Hail Mary full of grace the Lord be with you blessed are you among women and blessed is the fruit of thy womb Jesus and holy Mary mother of God pray for us sinners now at the hour of our death Amen.

I had the feeling of the thought of transcendence. I had the thought of the feeling of absolution. I had no idea what these words meant but they had popped up. I called one of my friends to ask what it meant and he told me . . . "I forgive you". I have to forgive myself. I have taken responsibility for me and I have now forgiven myself.

I have been given hope and now forgiveness is mine. As a child I would often wonder at the "H" in Anthony. Some people spell it without the "H" as is in mine and now I know what it stands for and that is HOPE.

I have hope today and live for the moment as this is all we have. I have given myself up to my higher power and I live with the warmth and knowledge that he is there for me, guiding me along my life's path. A path that will help others. I did it and if I can do it, so can you!

TONY—spelt backwards Y-NOT which means that there are NO boundaries, NO limits.

**You can do anything you really want to do and when you make your mind up to do it you will be helped along the way as I have.**

\*\*\*\*\*\*\*\*\*\*\*\*\*\*\*\*\*\*\*\*\*\*\*\*\*\*\*\*\*\*\*\*\*\*\*\*\*\*\*\*\*\*\*\*\*\*\*\*\*\*\*\*\*\*\*\*\*\*\*\*\*\*\*\*\*\*\*\*\*\*\*\*\*\*\*\*\*\*\*\*\*\*\*\*\*\*\*\*\*\*\*\*

# Short Stories Written by Tony— Twelve pennies

· · · · · · · · · · · · · · · · · · · · · · · · · · · · · · · · · · · · · · · · · · · · · · · · · · · · · ·

These short stories relate to the twelve pennies that I found at the hostel . . . a penny for your thoughts!!

## The Twelve Pennies

Do you believe in coincidences?

## The Number 27

There are many times that the number the number 27 has occurred in my life.

- In the year **2007** I had my last drink
- I was sent to prison for 27 months
- I had a vasectomy at the age of 27.

The list goes on. I know some may say that they may just be coincidences, but are they? This number keeps popping up in life and to give you an idea of what I mean I want to take you back to a time when I was enrolled on a 2 week course; what we call a 'back-to-work'—initiative program. I had been given a placement at Cadburys World and a time to start work. I decided to go to the train station the day before to find out the train times. It took **27** minutes to get there; the bus stop was outside the train station was the No **27** and so was the number of the bus. On arriving on my first day I was led to the reception area where I had been allocated a "buddy". A "buddy" was someone you could talk to whenever you had any problems. I was given a bus pass to get to work at the expense of Cadburys, for which I was grateful for. The serial number of the bus pass started with **27** and ended with **27**.

I was allocated to the "Cadburys Experience" department where I spent most of my time there showing people young and old onto the 'abra cadabra' ride and informing them about Cadburys. This took me back to a time when I was a juvenile at the Juvenile Court being in front of Lady Cadbury where she would have passed many sentences down on me over a period of time; a different ride altogether.

Today I give thanks to Lady Cadbury for the time she served me with and to pay back my gratitude for the time I spent at 'Cadburys Experience'. After completing my stint there and on my way home, I crossed the car park on foot and passed a mini car with the words **27** toms written on the side, I smiled and thought to myself how wonderful life was. On the train journey home it came into my mind that the housing benefit I received was **207** pounds.

A few days later I visited my friend, he invited me over as his mother had donated some clothes to a shop that I was help running; it was a charity shop for the homeless. Speaking to his mother for a while I made my leave, collecting the clothes on the way out Paul my friend asked me if I wanted a tennis racket I replied yes I picked it up and to my surprise written in bold was **27**.

I looked it up the meaning of the number 27 and found that in Greek numbers it is the 27th number of the alphabet which means dot, does that mean I am just a dot in time?

According to Feng Shui, to raise money, keep in the house 27 identical coins.

There is a greater meaning.... There are 27 books in the New Testament, *Revelation* being the twenty-seventh book; 27 Psalm

Whatever the meaning, it's what we take and learn from it that counts.

\*\*\*\*\*\*\*\*\*\*\*\*\*\*\*\*\*\*\*\*\*\*\*\*\*\*\*\*\*\*\*\*\*\*\*\*\*\*\*\*\*\*\*\*\*\*\*\*\*\*\*\*\*\*\*\*\*\*\*\*\*\*\*\*\*\*\*\*\*\*\*\*\*\*\*\*\*\*\*\*\*\*\*

## <u>Feelings</u>

One Tuesday morning I woke up feeling very well, and I decided to go to a "feelings meeting" over at Maypole. This is a place where I am able to relate the way that I feel in any one day and that day I was actually feeling very good.

After leaving the meeting a friend of mine called Luke gave me a lift back to Highgate. He dropped me off outside of the church. Looking up, I noticed that the name of the church was St. Luke's. Not knowing what direction I was going in, I walked down the street called Francis Street. That was the name of my father.

I reached a T-Junction and crossed over to Thomas Street. My name is Thomas. At the end of Thomas Street there were some gates to a park.

I entered the gates and sat on a bench, then all of a sudden without any warning, fear struck me as I was sat there. All my fears were there right in front of me. I was riveted to the bench. I just couldn't move and fear consumed me. I could hardly breathe. I gripped the bench so hard my knuckles were white. My heartbeat was so loud it deafened me. I was back to there, those time, those nightmares that I hoped I had left behind. They were here without any prompting or invitation they were upon me before I could even blink!

My nightmare of running to get away, running into the trees, running into everything, everywhere I ran I was blocked. The harder I ran the more I ran into things. The very beast I was running from was there breathing down my neck, reminding me, making me look, making me remember and there was no way out, no where safe to get to. Tears ran down my face. I was paralyzed with fear. Then all of a sudden a shaft of light appeared in my darkness, a gap in the trees, an escape route. My 12 Step Programme kicked in, and I thought phone my sponsor! As I took the phone from my pocket, a text came through from my, then, girlfriend. She asked me if I could get her some watermelons from the market. Ironically, that her maiden name was "Drinkwater" and her mum had just died from alcohol poisoning.

She lifted me from that park bench, it was like a hand reaching out to me in the darkness and I found that I could move and I made my way to the market for her! I bought her the melons that she'd asked for and I thanked her for doing this for me. She had given me a purpose, something I couldn't do for myself, and that led me back to her loving arms. A place of safety away from the beast, well at least for a while.

Days later, I was standing outside of the Swan Market in Erdington selling England tops to the public. I walked into a YMCA charity shop next to the Swan Market and I noticed a leather coat for sale for £7, and I asked if I could have it for £6, and they said "yes." I purchased the jacket and to my surprise on the back of the jacket in bold letters were the names, "Frank, Thomas." Ironically, they were the two streets that I had walked down that fearful day . . . Francis Street and Thomas Street!

\*\*\*\*\*\*\*\*\*\*\*\*\*\*\*\*\*\*\*\*\*\*\*\*\*\*\*\*\*\*\*\*\*\*\*\*\*\*\*\*\*\*\*\*\*\*\*\*\*\*\*\*\*\*\*\*\*\*\*\*\*\*\*\*\*\*\*\*\*\*\*\*\*\*\*\*

## <u>She</u>

This poem was written in 1980, whilst in Winson Green Prison. I was serving a 6 months prison sentence for dishonesty. The judge at Birmingham Crown Court also evoked my suspended sentence of 21 months running it consecutively with the 6 months therefore totalling 27 months in all. I am not saying I did not deserve it because I probably did without question.

This was an emotional time in my life. When I was being sentenced, I looked over the dock at, my then, girlfriend, and our eyes met. We both had tears rolling down our faces. That was the last time I was to see her as a single man. I will explain more as this unfolds further.

During the evenings when I was banged up in my cell, lonely and feeling very isolated, I used to listen to the radio, in particular a radio station called BRMB. Every Friday night without fail I would tune into a programme called "romantica". It used to play requests for inmates and partners who had requested certain songs for each other. It was a way of getting through the night and I fantasised over my girlfriend taking her into my arms and being affectionate with her, gently kissing her and telling her how much I loved her. The record at the time that used to take my fancy was "Betcha by Golly Wow" by the Stylistics. It was a sweet romantic melody and I was a romantic at heart. It brings tears to my eyes even today after 32 years. I compiled this poem from rearranged the words from another poem and adding a little to make it my own. I wrote to the radio station and requested the song above and asked them to play it for my girlfriend. To my sheer delight many weeks later I tuned in and to my surprise they read my poem out and played the record I requested. I was beside myself with joy and happiness and I could not wait to see my girlfriend and tell her. Hopefully she would have heard it too.

I wrote to her that night. I used to write to her on a daily basis. It was shortly afterwards on a visit that I told her about what had happened. She had heard about it from a friend of ours. She had gone out to the local pub the night it was played on air and she had been sitting with my dad!

Shortly after this I entered the poem into a contest at the prison education system and won second prize. The prize was a Mars bar and half an ounce of tobacco. I would have more than likely swapped the tobacco for something else as I don't smoke.

Not long after this I was summoned to the Governor's office and was informed that my application to marry had been given the go ahead and the date was set for the 20th of August 1980. I was over the moon and beside myself with joy. Who says prison is all doom and gloom. I always made the best of everything and accepted life for what it was. After all I did break the Law and I deserved to be where I was.

The day eventually came and I was transported to the church via taxi, handcuffed to a prison officer and another accompanied us to make sure that I got married. I do believe to this day that had I had not been in prison, I probably would not have got married. But hey, that's life. These things happen for a reason.

The officers were there to make sure I did not abscond and to make sure that I got me back to the prison. It was a simple ceremony. My mother and my sister were there and the prison escorts along with Father Fitzpatrick. Ironically I got married at St Patrick's Church. I wore clothes that were shoplifted and so were my brides. Hers was a maternity dress. You can blame me for the pregnancy but not for the theft of the clothes. I had a cast iron alibi! I was behind bars already!

After the ceremony, we went into a side room where the priest had prepared some sandwiches, tea and coffee. During all this time, the prison officers were keeping a close eye on me to make sure I did not make a run for it. Funny really that was exactly what my wife did over the 27 years we were married. I could never get away with anything. Yet today I am free to make my own choices in life.

Whilst eating a sandwich my mum pulled out of her bag a bottle of gin and asked me if I wanted to have a drink. I said "Mum put that away, have some respect. We are in church!" Yet an inner voice said "Go on, ask the priest. He won't mind." Even then there was an inner conflict going on. I succumbed and asked the priest to which he replied "Yes, but you had better ask the prison officers." Once again I asked the question "Do you mind boss?" leaning back in my chair, the handcuffs were off but I was manacled to the doors at the back of the room. I was going nowhere. They nodded at each other and one of them replied "As long as we can have one too". The bottle was opened and between the three of us there was not a drop left in the bottle. I was escorted back to prison and there I remained till I finished my sentence off.

I found out after that day that another prisoner had been unlawfully killed by certain officers working at the prison at that time. The prisoner at the time was on remand serving time for a domestic and drink related offence. I myself have been arrested many times for domestics concerning my wife and for the grace of God I am here to tell the story.

Looking back in hindsight to that day, I did get a glow and a warm feeling as I choose to believe it was because I got married in the house of God, to a lady that I should not have married. I am glad that I did marry her though because she gave me four wonderful sons and a beautiful daughter.

If I am honest, she probably kept me from the bottle more than I could ever realise. So with love in my heart I thank you my wife for the time and effort you gave me to keep me away from near death so many times over.

So to end this passage in time only this Alcoholic called Tony, could go into prison a single man, come out married with ten month old son.

AMEN

> **Her eyes are green, her lips are red and**
> **thoughts will ponder in her head**
>
> **She'll pace the floor and think out loud,**
> **devoted love to me she has vowed**
>
> **But I'm locked up and she is free and**
> **she'll stride about with fire and glee**

**But I'll write and she'll wait hoping**
**my letters are not too late**

**On receiving a letters she'll rush upstairs**
**and kneeling down she'll say her prayers**

**This time make sure she told herself and**
**took a pen down from the shelf**

**She'll write a letter to me in jail hoping**
**that I'll receive her mail**

**Onto her letters she'll write pleasant**
**dreams right through the night**

\*\*\*\*\*\*\*\*\*\*\*\*\*\*\*\*\*\*\*\*\*\*\*\*\*\*\*\*\*\*\*\*\*\*\*\*\*\*\*\*\*\*\*\*\*\*\*\*\*\*\*\*\*\*\*\*\*\*\*\*\*\*\*\*\*\*\*\*\*\*\*\*\*\*\*\*\*\*\*

## <u>The Red Lollipop</u>

I was talking with a friend in her home and I was being very suggestive with some of the stuff that I was saying to her when her young daughter tapped me on my shoulder, saying, "Hello, my name is Chloe." She obviously wanted some attention. So I turned and I looked at the lovely big smile on her face. I said to Chloe, "Get a piece of paper and draw me a picture of something that you want, and tell yourself everyday that you will get it, but it might not be on the day that you expect it."

Turning back to pick up the conversation where I had left off and I was just getting back into my groove, when I again felt a tap on my shoulder. Yes it was that lovely little Chloe again wanting more attention! She showed me the picture that she drawn and it was of a lollipop. I couldn't believe my eyes, it was the very same big red lollipop sitting on my coffee table at home. Someone had given to me the day before at work. I said in wonder "Chloe, you don't have to wait that long for that lollipop, because I have one at home just like that. You can have it." She smiled and I suggested that she should draw another picture and again turned back to my conversation. Yes, you guessed it, before long, a tap on the shoulder was felt again. Chloe showed me the picture that she had drawn, and this time it was a green tortoise and she had called it "Tony." I couldn't believe it! On the very same coffee table next to the lollipop, was a Christmas card which I had received from Bill, a rough sleeper, and on the card was a green tortoise called Tony!

I had been so grateful to Bill for having gone out and bought that card for me. He had taken the time and spent his little money on me. I have to this day still not brought the red lollipop over to Chloe, but I give my word that one day I will. I can learn a lot from Bill.

\*\*\*\*\*\*\*\*\*\*\*\*\*\*\*\*\*\*\*\*\*\*\*\*\*\*\*\*\*\*\*\*\*\*\*\*\*\*\*\*\*\*\*\*\*\*\*\*\*\*\*\*\*\*\*\*\*\*\*\*\*\*\*\*\*\*\*\*\*\*\*\*\*\*\*\*\*\*\*\*

## Trolleys

Walking down Common Lane on the way to work, I found myself being taken down a different route; it was a trip down memory lane. It took me back to a day in 1974 when I used to help my granddad and a man called John to sell fresh veg. The vegetables were from my granddad's garden and we used to place the produce in a trolley and pull it around the streets of Sparkbrook. Many fond memories attached to that trolley.

The thought of trolleys made me think of another trolley. It was 1976 and in was in borstal for young men who had committed crimes against society. I had been put to working cleaning pig sties at a farm and part of my duties were to look after the pigs and I had to use a trolley to pull the equipment needed to do that. I hated cleaning the pigs and one day I ran away from the farm and when I was found I took my punishment like a man; whipped with a wet towel. Not so fond memories with that one.

I then moved on to think about other trolleys that had played a part in my life. Interesting train of thought I know. It was then I remembered the time when I had been driving illegally around the streets of Nechells when one of the tyres punctured. Lucky for me I managed to pull up outside a garage where they maintained vehicles but it turned out not to be so lucky for them.

I asked if they could help me and a kind mechanic offered me the use of their trolley jack. I thanked him and took the trolley jack, jacked up the car, replaced the wheel and then swiftly put the trolley jack in the boot of the car and drove off. I had no thought or regard for the kindness of that man. I have come a long way since then.

My last encounter with a trolley was when I ended up in City hospital the day before my last drink. I was found drunk lying in the middle of the road causing a hazard to myself and others. I woke up on the trolley in the hospital. I did not want be admitted but I also didn't want to give up my trolley. Security was called and then there was a struggle. Next thing, I know, the police where bundling me into a police car and I taken to Rose Road Police Station where I was thrown into a cell. That was home for the rest of that night and the best part of the next day.

That was the last time I was involved with emergencies services. I was in a different place back then, over five years ago. You could say I have been off my trolley, pulled my trolley, been on my trolley and as long as I keep away from the drinks trolley I may end up with a trolley dolly. So here's to Frank dolly, cheers dad I love you.

On leaving work that day I changed back into my afternoon clothes and walked out the other side and into **Heart**lands Way!

\*\*\*\*\*\*\*\*\*\*\*\*\*\*\*\*\*\*\*\*\*\*\*\*\*\*\*\*\*\*\*\*\*\*\*\*\*\*\*\*\*\*\*\*\*\*\*\*\*\*\*\*\*\*\*\*\*\*\*\*\*\*\*\*\*\*\*\*\*\*\*\*\*\*\*\*\*\*\*

## Padre Pio

One day whilst talking with my sister, I noticed hanging on her wall a sketching of a man. It really caught my eye as it looked so much like our dad. It was uncanny. I asked her who drew the picture of dad and she replied she had found it hanging on a wall in a second hand shop. She had brought it because she too thought it resembled dad. I asked her if I could have it because at that time, I had no photos of dad. There were conditions! She stated that I was not to part with it and if I were to start drinking again I would have to give it back to her.

Many weeks later whilst sitting chatting with a friend, she noticed the same picture on the wall and asked who drew the picture of Padre Pio. I wondered what picture and who she was referring to until I realized she was looking at the picture my sister had given me. She was referring to the one that looked like my dad. She was quite amazed when I told her the story behind the picture and was adamant that it was a sketching of Padre Poi.

She went on to explain who Padre Pio was. He was the last living Saint who carried the wounds of Jesus Christ and carried the stigmata until he passed away peacefully at his church in San Giovanni in Southern Italy. I decided to go to visit of Padre Pio's shrine in San Giovanni and pay homage to his memory after doing a lot of research about his life.

Now here come some of those similarities that I am so fond of. I went on the 1.2.2011; paid £121 for the flight; came back on the 12.2 2011; my dad was born on the 2.2 1921; he passed away on the 1.2. 1989; my dads name was Frankie and Padre Pio's nick name was Frankie; his best friend was called Don and my sponsors name was Don. My grandmother's name was Bridget and Padre Pio's sister's name was Bridget. Lots of similarities don't you think?

I have compared a photo of myself, the one of my dad that I now have, and the sketching of Padre Pio. They look alike except for me, they both have a grey beard and both look like Father Christmas. It is ironic though that I can't grow a beard and I am clean shaven even at the age of 52 and that is just about the amount of years Padre Pio carried the wounds of Jesus.

I do not carry any such wounds and having reached the age of fifty two, I can honestly say that I am privileged to call myself an Alcoholic. I will always be an Alcoholic and will be until the the day die. I gave my sister my word and still to this day I have not touched a drop of alcohol. One day at a time sweet Jesus and that picture still has pride of place on my wall.

\*\*\*\*\*\*\*\*\*\*\*\*\*\*\*\*\*\*\*\*\*\*\*\*\*\*\*\*\*\*\*\*\*\*\*\*\*\*\*\*\*\*\*\*\*\*\*\*\*\*\*\*\*\*\*\*\*\*\*\*\*\*\*\*\*\*\*\*\*\*\*\*\*\*\*\*\*\*\*\*\*\*\*

## **Forgotten Vintage**

I myself had been rendered homeless through issues that I have come to terms with and are still coming to terms with on a daily basis. I had reach a point in my life where it was time for me to give back which had been given to me; the much needed time support, resources and kindliness.

You cannot put a price on what was given but this was my way of saying thank you. I was working as a volunteer in a shop called Forgotten Vintage. This shop was a Social Enterprise created by Reach and Sifa-Fireside, two homeless Charities trying to raise much needed funds to tackle the issues of homelessness. My gratitude for what has been given to me and the life I live today has to be given freely and with no expectations.

The day after the launch of the shop and I was folding up t-shirts which had been created by the homeless people to promote awareness of their plight when a realization came into my head. I had been praying that one day that I would come into some money and be able to open a shop and sell second hand goods. As a child I had always dreamed of being in a western. Here I was in the Great Western Arcade selling second hand clothing with my cowboy boots under the table and there on the wall was a picture of me with a cowboy hat on with the headlines saying "**Second Chance for Tony**". I should be grateful it wasn't a 'WANTED' poster.

So there you have it through prayer and meditation without putting my hands in my pocket I have become a Deputy for my Sheriff and I carry his message . . . that the power of prayer and thought for others will make you a star.

A year later the shop has become a vital resource within the heart of the City, I really do enjoy spending a lot of my spare time there and as a result of my volunteering there I have been given a job in the city at Washing Court a hostel for many outlaws as I was once myself. So you could say I have been given many rewards since putting down the drink and there is no bounty on my head, so for now I am at my own ok korral and enjoy being on the bandwagon.

\*\*\*\*\*\*\*\*\*\*\*\*\*\*\*\*\*\*\*\*\*\*\*\*\*\*\*\*\*\*\*\*\*\*\*\*\*\*\*\*\*\*\*\*\*\*\*\*\*\*\*\*\*\*\*\*\*\*\*\*\*\*\*\*\*\*\*\*\*\*\*\*\*\*\*\*\*\*\*\*\*\*\*

## **<u>Never a Full Shilling</u>**

Walking down Tennal Road after just being asked to leave my girlfriend's home because we had just had words and I was tearful and slightly upset. Not really knowing why, I started to think, when all of a sudden a thought came into my head. As a result of these steps came these principles to all of my affairs. I repeated it over and over again in my head. The penny dropped. It was like a cascade of pennies, like I had just won the jackpot.

Earlier that morning I was at SIFA Fireside doing volunteering for the homeless sorting out clothes for the shop in town called the Forgotten Vintage. I placed my hand in the bottom of a bag and I felt a load of coins. Grabbing hold of all of them I counted twelve coins, twelve old pennies to be precise, which is the equivalent of a full shilling, I'm not saying that I'm a full shilling but that's what they are equivalent to. I thought to myself that I had been given a penny for every step that I had done in the Twelve Step Program of recovery that I live my life by. "Bingo," I thought, I have had a spiritual awakening and my awareness is aware of me.

A few days later I was at an event at SIFA Fireside, it was a celebration of thirty years of homeless on the streets of Birmingham. One of the events that was going on was an enactment of Oliver with some of service users that use the services of Sifa as I did over a four year period. Now I am part of the structure as a volunteer and I am part of the fund raising committee. I have many other roles there and in each and every role I play in life I am playing myself. Oliver was played acted out by the service users, as I was one once and could be if I was ever to pick up a drink, but not today thank you. I never picked a pocket and took pennies off anybody. I did do many dishonest things in my life but as result of the way I live my life today, I am an honest person.

Sitting on a bus many days later, somebody tapped me on the shoulder and asked me how I was doing, I did not recognize him and asked who he was and he replied that he knew me from a time I went to a rehab centre to share my experience strength and hope with a group of drunks. His name was Oliver. I asked him how he was doing and he went on to reply that he had had a slip and was trying to get his life back on track. We chatted for awhile and exchanged phone numbers; I did call him a few times later and prayed for him occasionally and I do hope he is okay. I do hope to see Oliver again in the near future, clean and sober and not dirty and black like one of the characters in Oliver twist.

\*\*\*\*\*\*\*\*\*\*\*\*\*\*\*\*\*\*\*\*\*\*\*\*\*\*\*\*\*\*\*\*\*\*\*\*\*\*\*\*\*\*\*\*\*\*\*\*\*\*\*\*\*\*\*\*\*\*\*\*\*\*\*\*\*\*\*\*\*\*\*\*\*\*\*\*\*\*\*\*

## **Mine Sacred Heart**

Walking up Edward's Road one day many years ago, with not a thought in my head, when I started thinking to myself 'in my red case earth', 'in my red case earth'. True to character I jumbled up these words and rearranged them to say "Mine Sacred Heart," Anyone could do that with an anagrammed mind.

An anagram is a word that can be jumbled up and rearranged into another word and I had grandma in anagram and I never knew a grandma in my life, but I must have had one because I came to believe her name was Bridget. Now anybody could do that and rearrange the words, but could they do this, walking down Edward's Road a different day to the day I was walking up, more or less parallel to meeting myself, where I stopped at a garage and there was gentleman selling bric-a-brac. I stopped and rummaged through the bits and piece that he had and bought ten cards from him, these were cards with names and the meanings of names, and as I looked down at the right hand side on the floor there was a large red case. I asked how much the case was, and he replied "Just a pound." I gave him the pound, thanked him and left and then walked the remainder to my home carrying my case. Sitting on the edge of my bed I opened up the case and there was nothing in it. So I thought to myself, "It is up to me to put something in it," but I had nothing, but I had everything really, and I had it all in abundance. I then a thought came into my head, I would put my dad's death certificate and his birth certificate which I had sent off to an insurance company who were dealing with the claim for an inheritance which I had came into. I was waiting for these to be returned to me, but they had been lost in transit and I was trying to contact the postal services and the insurance company to find out their whereabouts. As I thought this I heard something drop to the floor, so I got up, I walked into the kitchen, and there on the floor was some mail which had been posted through my kitchen window, as I didn't have a mailbox at that time. The lady in front of the house had posted my mail through as my mail gets delivered through her letterbox. The lady's name was Vicky, she had four boys, my wife had four boys from me. Vicky had a red focus car, and I also had had a focus car. She had a red boxer dog, and I also had had a red boxer dog. Vicky's next door neighbours are called Tommy and Kathleen, my name is Thomas and my mother's name was Kathleen. Tommy and Kathleen were also the chief executors into the state of the inheritance which I had came into and were also cousins of mine and lived next door to my granddad in the early '70s in a place so similar to the home that I was living in today. On the other side of the house from where I was living there had just moved in a young couple, their names were Gary Ellor and his wife's name was Anita. I at that time had been married to my wife whose name was Anita, coincidental or was it meant to be just to remind me of my past life? Picking up the letters from the floor I went and sat on my bed, opening up the mail to my amazement were the death certificate and the birth certificate which I thought had got lost in the post and there they were before my very eyes. Looking at the death certificate I noticed the time of my dad's passing, I lived at 19 Hornsey Road, Kingstanding, B44 so be there for what do I do with the other four? I place it next to the one nine, making one nine four. It was only the combination of the lock on the red suitcase in front of me. On the handle of the suitcase there was a band and on the band there were four things written, first was "Tom," but my name is Thomas, but it had obviously been to Thompson's Airways. Second was "Man," well I was a man the last time I checked my credentials, but it had obviously been to Manchester Airport. Third was the "18th February," it had obviously flown into or out of the country on the 18th February, which happens to be my date of birth. Fourth was "204," so if I take out the nothing I have made something out of nothing, that leaves twenty four and I live at B24. I live on Orchard Road and I actually have six apple trees and three blackberry bushes in my garden, so I actually live in an orchard. My last drink was Scrumpy Cider which is supposed to be made out of apples and my postcode is 121 Orchard Road, Erdington, B24 9JE so I have a one to one with my higher power and if I put the nine which could be an S next to JE could be I'm living in Jesus' domain. I know this is only relevant to me, but I am aware of it, and it keeps me sober on a daily basis. Every time I walk up and down Edward's Road, I walk past a shop called Brew Genie, which sells apparatus for making your own brew. I could if I wanted buy some apparatus and take the apples from the tree and brew my own cider and live hell on earth but I would rather leave the apples where they are and live in heaven on earth.

\*\*\*\*\*\*\*\*\*\*\*\*\*\*\*\*\*\*\*\*\*\*\*\*\*\*\*\*\*\*\*\*\*\*\*\*\*\*\*\*\*\*\*\*\*\*\*\*\*\*\*\*\*\*\*\*\*\*\*\*\*\*\*\*\*\*\*\*\*\*\*\*\*\*\*\*\*\*\*\*\*\*\*\*

## Chocolate

I was lying in bed one Friday evening a few years ago; when it suddenly dawned on me that it was actually Good Friday. My grandchildren came into my head, Kirsty and Cameron. I thought to myself how nice it would be to go and see them on Easter Sunday and buy them an Easter egg, as I had not done this for many a year. I pondered this thought and fell into a nice sleep and woke up the next morning feeling fresh. I said my prayers and left my home with a good feeling I would see my grandchildren the next day. My first stop of the day was to have breakfast at Wilton market, on the way in I noticed that my friend Frank had set up a stall outside selling Easter eggs, he had four or five pallets of them and one day to sell them. I greeted him and wished him the best of luck; I did notice some large eggs amongst them and thought how nice it would be to purchase two of them for Kirsty and Cameron. After eating my breakfast, I went about my daily business and returned back to the market about three o clock, when one of Franks employees came up to see me and said to me that Frank wanted a word with me. Speaking to Frank he said that he hadn't done very well selling the eggs and could I sell them for him, as I had the gift of the gab for I had been a market trader most of my life. He told me that he would give me a drink if I done well selling the eggs I replied I don't drink, and if he was to give me two of the large eggs I would try and sell them. If I sold one all of them or any amount in between all I wanted was the two large eggs, he agreed we shook hands and I commenced to what I do best. I scrambled up a crowd and was selling the eggs at quite a good rate always offering a good deal to the crowd. Making them smile and sending them home with a bargain. Couple of hours later time was running out and we finished selling with only half a pallet left, every body was more than satisfied and as agreed Frank gave me the two eggs and on the table I noticed three eggs in cups wrapped up in nice wrapping paper. I asked Frank if I could also have them, he agreed and I placed them carefully with the other eggs. I was amazed when etched on the cups was woody from toy story a film narrated by Tom Hanks, re-arranged spells Thomas K which is my name, it leaves an N placed in the word toy spells Tony. So there you have it Tony story. I left the market and caught a bus to town and sat at the front of the bus a young lady got on with her little boy, he smiled at me looked at the eggs and smiled at me again. I asked his mother if I could give one of the eggs to him, she agreed and thanked me as did the little boy he was gleaming with happiness. I struck up a conversation with his mother and to my surprise I found out she lived with my son Anthony. We got off in town and went our different ways. Standing at another bus stop in town a lady next to me asked what I had in the bags I was carrying, I replied Easter eggs, she asked if she could have one I gave her one and we chatted. I told her I was a recovering Alcolic in recovery, she told me that her brother was suffering from this illness and I suggested that he went to fellowship I belong to. She thanked me and I went on my way when I met a lady I know coming out of a door carrying a large bottle of cider. I greeted her and asked how her son Tommy was doing, she said he was doing fine and was at home safely tucked up in bed. I gave her the remaining egg for her son and wished her good night. Ironic his name was Tom and his dad was in prison and his dads name was Tom also. Visiting my grand children the next day I gave them their Easter eggs and related most of what I have wrote and my grand daughter chipped in you're a bit of a smarty pants granddad so you are, we all laughed and enjoyed the rest of the day. So you could say life is like a box of chocolates as Forest Gump quoted.

**************************************************************************

## Fob watches

I woke up one morning a few years ago at the Lincoln Poacher a pub I was managing for a friend of mine. I noticed that, the drawers to the sideboard where open, looking over I also noticed that they looked as if they had been rifled through. This is where I kept my personal belongings and amongst them were my dad's fob watches and these were missing. I had given these to my dad back in the days when he was alive and when he passed away they had been returned back to me for keeps sake. A memory had came back to me of a time when I had stolen one of the watches and had probably bought the other with stolen money I never did tell my dad how I came by them, he accepted them with pride and wore them proudly. Getting dressed and probably upset with the thought of somebody stealing them I placed my hand in my pocket and to my surprise I pulled out the watches which were in a money bag to keep them in good condition. Baffled by their re-appearance a thought came to me that perhaps I had rifled the drawers in my sleep and took the watches like I was enacting my past and to do this it had pricked my conscience. Straight away I knew what I had to do and that was to return them to the rightful owners, but how could this be possible I though have between me and my dad I had these watches nearly forty years. I know I said to myself I will hand them into the police at the nearest convenient time. Later on in the afternoon I was speaking to my friend and had related to him the morning events and what I had proposed to do about it, he suggested that I hand them into the police station and say that I had found them. I told him that would still be lying and that I must be truthful, he told me that I was off my head and to do whatever made me feel better and went his way.

Later on in the evening I was looking after a little boy called Alex and decided to take him to the shop to buy him some sweets, he led the way to the shop and I followed behind. Reaching the shop a police car pulled up and two police officers got out and entered the shop and me and Alex followed on behind them. With out a thought I walked up to one of the police officers and took out the watches from my pocket and told them what I had told my friend, the police officer told me what my friend had told me and if I wanted to make an issue out of it I could get arrested. With concern for Alex I placed the watches back in my pocket bought Alex some sweets and left the shop feeling a lot better than when I did going in. The police officer looked at me with a puzzled expression like I was trying to fob him off.

\*\*\*\*\*\*\*\*\*\*\*\*\*\*\*\*\*\*\*\*\*\*\*\*\*\*\*\*\*\*\*\*\*\*\*\*\*\*\*\*\*\*\*\*\*\*\*\*\*\*\*\*\*\*\*\*\*\*\*\*\*\*\*\*\*\*\*\*\*\*\*\*\*\*\*\*\*\*\*\*\*\*\*\*

## Bananas

One Sunday morning I had slept in late and on awakening I said my prayers and asked my god to guide me through the day. I came to a decision that I would go to a meeting in Newtown, a meeting I had been to many times before but in a different direction. I walked up to six ways in Erdington and caught the number eleven bus to Witton where I was going to get the number seven bus to Newtown. I got off the number eleven bus at Witton Island and walked a little way towards the number seven bus. I walked into a shop on the way and decided to buy myself a banana offering the money to the Asian gentleman behind the counter he said that I could have it without paying for it, I thought to myself what a kind man. I thanked him and left the shop, peeling the banana and feeling free I walked up a street I once lived as a teenager and stood out side the door I once lived at. Silently praying and thanking God for the home I lived in at that time, directly facing my home at that time was a home of a lady called Mrs Murphy. I had befriended this Lady and used to run errands for her and some times short changing her and stealing from her bag. Guilt and remorse returned back to me and I was tearful, other memories came flooding back of the times of the beatings that I used to take, in particular from an Asian man strapping me to a lamp post whilst passersby's passed on by perhaps this was in a way poetic justice for the wrongs I caused others. I do accept this was the case but there was a sense of injustice in it all has where ever I went beatings followed me like the plague. Tears flowed from my eyes at the memories, saying the serenity prayers many times over I gained control of my emotions. The number seven pulled up I got on and seated myself at the front of the bus. Oblivious to everything I heard a woman call out to the person in front of her 'have you ever drank in the Barton Arms? I thought to myself I had many times and looking over at her I was startled to know and recognise as a flower seller who sellers her flowers outside the rag market in town and her name is Kate Kelly which so happens to be the name of my mum and resembled Mrs Murphy. She was talking about Big Jean from the block of flats nearby and my sister Jean passed away eighteen months ago and I believe she has gone to god's mansion and is awaiting my arrival. Tears started rolling again and I got off the bus in a sorrowful state crying uncontrollably, three men happened to get off the bus that I knew from the fellowship I belonged to and hugged me and told me everything would be o.k. So from going bananas to loving you have made me bananas.

# Afterword from Tracy

· · · · · · · · · · · · · · · · · · · · · · · · · · · · · · · · · · · · · · · · · · · ·

Well, the story has been told and hopefully you will have taken something of value from reading all about Tony's last drink. I know that I have! I learnt a lot from him too. I am not just referring to this chapter in his life and his dance with alcohol and alcoholism but the man himself. Tony is far more than a recovering alcoholic; he is a man of great inspiration and honour. Even with 32 convictions, he has shown how deep this honour is embedded. Even in his darkest moments he showed his true inner being. He reached out to help someone when his own world was crumbling around his ears and there seemed no hope. The 'light' within was always there, it just had not had the opportunity to shine for others to see. Mind you, for people to have seen this they need to have their eyes open and a non judgemental attitude of mind. Acceptance is the key to achieving this and for some that is a step too far. Some people find it very difficult to actually love and accept themselves and who they truly are. Some are even afraid of finding out what their true essence is and hide in the shadows of their souls never to step out into the sunshine of what their true essence is. Tony took that inward look and found something worth saving and even in his darkest hour he found the strength from somewhere to take the necessary step forward. If Tony can do it, so can you. He accepted that he had allowed himself to be led down a path of pain and destruction that lost him everything and hurt many people on the way. Even more, he accepted that his behaviour was no longer acceptable and that changes had to be made and 'God' became his guiding light along with the Fellowship. It is important for you to realize, and it is something that I believe in, that is people are not their behaviour. Behaviour is the result of many internal and external factors, but it is not the person and who they truly are. It is not their essence. We can all have days where we are a bit crabby and unreasonable when we are having a bad day, but it does not alter our true being. Tony started his journey of self discovery when he called out in the early hours that dark and dreary day and with each step he learnt so much about himself. With each little step and even the backward steps he started to forgive and love himself and that gave him the strength to face his demons and keep moving forward. It did not matter whether those steps brought pain or joy he took them and that was all that really mattered. We are all on a journey and if you stop life stagnates and you could miss so much of what life really has to offer you. Tony did not stand still, he refused to be held prisoner by the drink and turned round to his demons and said 'Enough! No more!' He keeps taking those steps forward and is not afraid to face life and all that it has in store. Life is for living and that is exactly what Tony is doing and I salute him! Well done my dear friend for it is a courageous act that you carried out and so empowering. I know he would say it's not courageous but it is as many would have not taken on the battle. It would have seemed too daunting to even think about it and it would have been so easy just to let the demons consume your very being and give up the fight. Tony didn't give up and I am so glad that he turned round and faced the challenge life presented for I would not have had the privilege of getting to know him. He has been a guiding light not just for me but for many people and I know this for a fact as I have heard people say it with my own ears!

During my time in working with Tony, he has taken me on a journey that I never expected to take or even experience and I thank him with all my heart. Tony, you took my hand and showed me the echoes of your past memories and the very dark crevices deep within your being. I sensed the pain and the feeling of total abandonment along with the self-loathing and disgust of whom and what you had become. It was as if I was revisiting a time and place of years gone by and looking through your eyes and living those scenes that were presented before me. I even felt the draw and power of the light that guided you back to your divine purpose in life. It led us both; it took us away from the abyss of darkness and back into the light and showed us the way. It illuminated the pathway to ensure that each step was taken safely and in the direction that we should and must take. That force shines bright in Tony's life and he has now become part of that light and I too am still touched by it even now.

Whilst researching more about alcoholism, Tony was kind enough to invite me to some of the meetings that he regularly attends. I met such wonderful and inspiring people at these meetings and I would like to take this opportunity to thank them for welcoming me into the fold and sharing their darkest moments with me. In addition to my thanks I would like to add that 'you' are all so much more than recovering alcoholics. Alcoholism is just a part of you, okay it may be a powerful part, but you are all so much more and my wish is that you all start to see the other many special qualities that you all possess and celebrate them. You have had the strength of character to turn your back on alcohol and its hold over you. That was 'you', not the alcoholic part of you, it was the others parts of you that make the whole.

There have been many things that have stood out to me over the last few months whilst on this journey and probably one of the biggest things is that the 12 Steps and the principals behind them encourage people to live for the moment. I celebrate this fact and endorse it 100%. It is a shame that some people have to experience so much pain and destruction with alcoholism before they do, yet they DO truly live for the moment and in the moment. They are living their life and feeling the pain and the joy that goes with it and accepting themselves for who they are. If you were to sit quietly in a public place and watch the people going about their daily business you will start to become aware of how many people are just going through the motions. They are just existing and not truly living. They walk around with closed eyes and heavy hearts on auto-pilot. These are probably the same people that frown at alcoholism and condemn alcoholics. They could learn so much from the Principals of the 12 Step Program. I felt humbled and moved, sometimes to the point of tears during the Fellowship Meetings for I witnessed with my own eyes another human being reaching out with love and understanding to someone that had stumbled and fallen on the path of life. I don't mean just one person reaching out, but the whole group! The sense of love and compassion for someone who had fallen to depths that many of us don't even know exist and the reaching out of a helping hand to help them back up on their feet was unbelievable. The whole experience has restored my faith in mankind.

I deeply wish that after reading Tony's story that you will take the time to step back, even for a moment, and look at your own life. View it with open eyes and with true honest vision. See the changes that you know are needed so that you can actually start living the life you truly desire.

Take responsibility for your life. Stop acting the victim and take control. Your life starts with you and ends with you with everything in between being your responsibility. Start living for the moment and feel how good it is to be present in your own life.

**Why Not? Tony did!**

# A message from Tony

· · · · · · · · · · · · · · · · · · · · · · · · · · · · · · · · · · · · · · · · · · · · · · · · ·

**Where is Tony today?** Well, I am right here where I am supposed to be at this very moment. I am here lying in my own bed in my own home in Orchard Street putting together the pieces of my life over the last 5 year for the finishing touches to my book. A book that I have created for all those still suffering people on the streets of Birmingham. So to bring about a greater awareness of the homeless and what it is really all about.

Life is a journey and it's what we learn on that journey that matters. The wisdom and knowledge gained during my journey has been and will continue to be shared with you and I hope after reading this you feel you can do the same. On that glorious day, not so long ago, the day of my last drink, which I must say only seems like yesterday yet a million miles away from where I am today; I smile to myself as I think of The Beatles song "Imagine"; just imagine this book becoming an overnight sensation and being able to reach out to others and inspire them to take the first steps to a new beginning. Amazing! From that last drink I ventured out of my world into the real world. A world that I have come to realize was and has always been, all around me yet not visible. The start of my journey took me to the other side of town to the charitable organization called Sifa-Fireside; a drop-in centre for the Homeless. They fed me, clothed me and developed me. They nurtured the child within so I could grow into the man that you see today. My self confidence was brought to life through the development courses and various activities that were bestowed upon me by the organization. This enabled me to ignite the fires of self belief.I go back even today to my starting point and use their services regularly, but in a different way than I did back then. I became a Volunteer and found a way of giving back for what was given to me. Working in the community meant I had another opportunity to go back to Cadbury's for two weeks. Lady Cadbury had been there for me when I was a young delinquent and I had faced the music many a time and now it was time to say 'thank you'. I didn't know then how grateful I would be for all that had happened and for the things that keep happening along my journey. All good things were happening and humility became a natural everyday process in my life. The wheel of life kept turning and I moved from volunteering to a six month contract with 'Inspired Futures'. While I was contracted there I helped people put together their CV's and action plans whilst providing positive feedback into a better way of being. I find this quite ironic when I review the past, for now for my future I want to inspire others. I want to be an inspiration for change, for if I can say that this is what I have done with my life, then you can do it too. Only the other week I was part of the interview panel for a secure unit called the Tamering Centre and now 5 Years on I am a Support Worker for Trident for 'Reach the People Charity'. This has always been something I have wanted to do. These charities for the homeless when I was on the streets of Birmingham, gave me hope and a wealth of opportunities. The work that I am doing now is work that I love doing and I even get paid for it! What a bonus. Someone once said to me that if you find a job you love doing then you will never have to work again for the rest of your life. I Love what I am doing and I keep on doing what I love. I do it because it was done for me and for a lifetime from the point of being born to where I am today I am grateful. I do not use the word 'grateful' lightly. I truly mean 'grateful'! I have a lot of good things in my life and I appreciate all that I have and have had and the things that are yet to come.Over those last 5 years I have done many course and received many awards for changing my life around. I have been into schools and universities delivering and facilitating Homeless awareness through my work that I do now. I have been to Italy on a spiritual adventure for 12 days and went to see the shrine of Padre Pio and spent six days in Rome visited the Vatican. The list is endless of the places I have visited and experienced and now my world is getting bigger and I have so much more to see and do. In this short period of time I have done more, learnt more and love life so much more than I ever did in my previous 47 years. Before I was in a place where I just existed and dreams where a waste of inner resources. The most valuable lessons I have learnt *is to love rather than be loved; to understand rather than to be understood; to have faith rather than to fear; to console rather than to be consoled.* I thank God every single day for every day that I have and every day is a blessing. At the moment I have had few days of going through some emotional pain and I have never felt pain like it. The difference today is that I do not drink on it! I choose to share it with others and that is what takes the pain away. I would rather feel it, live it, share it and let go of it and give it to God. The last thing on my mind today is to drink. It's like I never drank at all. I have to remind myself every day through prayer and meditation of that last drink and have come to realize that it was the best drink I ever drank. I would not have what I have today if it was not for that last drink and I only have it today and that brings peace of mind. Not many people can say that they have 'peace of mind' for it is so rare and precious and I would rather give up this life than trade it for one lousy drink! Saying thank you is very important to me and I have so many people I want to thank. I will not name you all for you know who you are and I would hate to leave anyone out. However I feel compelled to say a big thank you to Sifafireside and the many other services down the line that have helped me to get where I am today and a special thanks to Tracy my co-creator. One person I would like to give special thanks to Dr Wayne Dyer for his inspirational work that has been the key to finding me. I truly hope to meet this wonderful man for he taught me that a problem is only a problem if you say it's a problem. If you think it's a problem, you think more a problem of it. Change the way you are thinking, be positive.I have one more thank you to share with you. I thank God for the things and the people that have been put in my path along this journey of rediscovery. A journey that will take me to a better world and that world is out there. It's out there for everyone if they care to find the key to open the door to themselves. So whenever you are struggling or suffering and you say to yourself 'why me?' why me?' stop and think 'Why not? If Tony can do it so can I!' I am hoping that this book can reach out to others. I am just a little boy at heart who has found his way through that dark. I have stumbled along the tunnel of darkness with just one ray of light to guide me on my way and that ray of light I choose to call God. To my family and friends and to my little sister who passed away; who I believe is waiting for me on the other side with our mom and dad, I have more work to do for God so wait for me and to all the people living on the streets anywhere in the world, God blesses you all.

Lightning Source UK Ltd.
Milton Keynes UK
UKOW05f1028310713

214656UK00002B/154/P